BUILDING SELF-CONFIDENCE

Learn to live life feeling strong, confident and self-assured.

By

Andrew Stanton

Table of Contents

Introduction

Welcome to your first issue of Building Self Confidence. In each issue of Building Self Confidence, you will learn valuable information on how you can successfully build your self-confidence and live life feeling strong, confident and self-assured

Chapter 1

Signs of Low Self-confidence and How You Can Recognize Them, Begin to Conquer Self-doubt.

We are going to talk about the signs of low self-confidence and how you can recognize them and begin to conquer self-doubt. While there is no single factor that leads to a lack of confidence.

Most often, it is the accumulation of negative experiences from our past, which we fail to deal with when they happen. It is also the result of our failure to recognize who we truly are and what hinders our growth.

Low self-confidence is defeating. It can define us and cause us to beat ourselves up emotionally. It can limit our abilities and keep us from growing and moving forward from our mistakes, failures and defeats.

It confines us to our comfort zone where everything is safe from potential humiliation and further mistakes. We then are stuck in that comfort zone believing that we shouldn't move away from it because if we do we will only be left hurt and disappointed.

Once you are stuck in that zone, it is very hard to move forward in life, which keeps us from achieving our dreams, reaching our goals and living a rich full life. Even when we tell ourselves that no matter how harsh and messed up things get, we shouldn't surrender to the inner critic that thrives inside us we are still filled with self-doubt and a profound lack of confidence.

Low self-confidence usually develops during our childhood. Unfortunately, many of us have family, teachers, friends and enemies who are more than happy to point out our mistakes and/or faults rather than praising our talents.

They may not even realize what they're doing or how big an impact they are having on your self-confidence. They may not even say anything to your face, but often their actions speak louder than words, which makes us feel inadequate and worthless early on in our developmental years.

Perhaps you live under the cold critical eyes of someone who doesn't see the good in anything. Maybe you are related to an overachiever and live in the shadow of their accomplishments. Perhaps those around you make you feel like you can't do anything right. These are all triggers that can make you feel inferior and inadequate which only adds to your lack of confidence.

With poor rule models and lack of support, many grow up feeling as if they are incapable of doing certain things, growing and achieving anything of value. When in fact each of us has our inner strength and power to take control of our lives. We just have to have the confidence to do it.

Once you recognize the underlying causes of your lack of confidence, you can begin the process of overcoming the impact it has on your life. The best place to start is by evaluating the triggers that smash your confidence and make you feel inadequate. A good place to start is by keeping a journal.

Write down times when you're feeling less than confident and what caused you to feel that way. You should also write down things that you could do differently that will help make you feel better and more confident about yourself. By identifying these triggers and combating them with positive reinforcement, you can begin to move forward and become the self-confident person inside you.

Chapter 2

Building Self Confidence

In the last Chapter, we talked about the signs of low self-confidence. In this issue, we are going to go over some different ways that you can increase your self-confidence

Don't be fooled. Even the most confident people have their insecurities and the people who appear extremely self-confident aren't perfect. No one is!

Even though we dream of being perfect and we see other people who appear self-confident and all together, we have to realize that no one can be perfect. We are all human and we all make mistakes. The things we want to happen in our lives don't necessarily happen the way we want them to, no matter how carefully we plan our futures. The things we want to achieve will pass us by when we don't work towards achieving them. It takes effort and self-confidence to make things happen.

Even the most confident person doesn't become that way by sheer luck people. They have to work at it. Someone once said that the most successful people don't just happen. They must know hardship, they must know suffering, they must know defeat, struggle and loss before they truly understand the depth of their worth.

Everyone is built for recognition, achievement, for fame. The capacity to be confident in oneself does not happen by chance, it lies within all of us. Like with all other things in life we are just as capable as the person sitting next to us. The only difference is our belief in ourselves and that we can accomplish anything we set our minds to.

As we discussed in the last topic, a lack of self-confidence can stem from our childhood, is impacted by the people around us and determines how we grow up as well as what we achieve. At a very young age, we already know the difference between being humiliated or encouraged. We already understand when good or bad things happen to us.

During childhood, if we are lost to react positively to negative situations whether it's due to the lack of or proper guidance, support or poor role models, it’s likely that the succeeding phases of our lives will become dependent on how things went during our formative years.

However, with age comes maturity and maturity comes from the experiences we go through. Experience is one of the greatest teachers we have. Failure to learn from the experiences we encounter only keeps us reliving the same types of situations until we’re able to see where we’ve gone wrong and stop the cycle of self-defeat.

Improving self-confidence is just a matter of becoming more mature and learning from our mistakes. Everyone can improve his or her self-confidence regardless of how we were in the past. What matters is now, the present. If you take stock of yourself and believe that you can be anything and everything you want to be, you can move towards achieving your dreams and becoming more self-confident.

There are many ways to help you improve your self-confidence. The key is to have a positive attitude and remember that you can do anything you set your mind to.

More About Increasing Your Self-confidence.

Confidence lies in our perception of ourselves. The difference between being afraid to try and being confident in your abilities comes with our understanding and acceptance of the experiences we go through in life. Some people are just better at recognizing their abilities and achieving their goals than others are.

Like being rich, we think that self-confidence is something that everyone has, except us. When in fact we were all created equal and have the power within us to achieve anything. Inequality just comes with our notions of what we already have and fail to recognize positively.

To overcome a lack of confidence it's important not to be too hard on yourself when things don't go as well as expected. Don't deprive yourself of enjoying life. Take stock of yourself and refrain from making excuses as to why you can reach your goals. Instead, change your mindset and think of all of the positive things in your life and how you achieved them.

Many of us find ourselves limited by our experiences. However, that doesn't mean we can't learn grow from those experiences and change our perception of ourselves. We are all gifted with certain talents, skills and beauty within along with the power to use or disregard them. Once we recognize our potential, we will find that life has much more to offer than mediocrity.

Generally, self-confidence and how we improve it is achieved only when we dare to do things that are out of our comfort zones. We sometimes fail to recognize that simple things like reflecting on our achievements can help improve our level of confidence.

We can build our self-confidence in a multitude of ways. Activities like developing your verbal skills through writing and public speaking will help increase your sense of self. Many of us have a fear of speaking in public. Once you take the steps to conquer this fear, you will discover that your confidence will increase, and even more, is possible. This holds for any fear you may have. Once you make up your mind not to let it beat you a world of possibilities will open. By recognizing that life holds endless possibilities and you just have to be open to them, you can take control of your life and be a strong and confident person capable of accomplishing anything.

Chapter 3

How Your Inner Critic Affects Your Self-confidence.

It is strange how many of us fail to listen to that tiny voice inside ourselves. There is no biological or scientific explanation for this voice, but we all hear them. An innate murmuring voice telling us we aren't good enough, we're worthless, we can't do anything right, does this sound familiar?

For some, the voice is the all-commanding mentor and for some, this little voice has become their inner critic or worse a guiding force in their lives. If we would all remember, this tiny voice has been with us throughout our lives, guiding us to make the proper decisions.
But during life, when we have become too jaded and have forgotten the beliefs we once had, this voice becomes silent that we no can no longer remember how good it feels to listen to its guidance. It was intended to help us but our negative thoughts turn that little voice into an inner critic.

This inner critic is the nagging voice that tells you how deficient you are, how ugly you are, how weak and useless you are and how people dislike you for who and what you are. It will convince you to believe in all these lies until your self-confidence is sapped and your sense of self becomes devoid.

You may try not to listen to this inner critic initially. Yet once you believe in its miserable denials of who you are, you are sure to have it win you over. You will then be convinced of the validity of its claims and so, you will resort to succumbing to mediocre and somber life.

This inner critic lives in all of us as much as the inner voice of goodness does. Theirs is a battle to conquer your being. To deliver you back from the course of goodness and happiness or to the other end.

This inner critic will provide proof of how stupid it would be to take chances with faith. It will create a proof of how unable and incapacitated you are against shining. It will make you believe in time that you truly are worthless and insignificant.

It will store memories of such failures to be recovered when you falter with "unbelief". This inner critic will eat you up until it overpowers your sense of self. You will eventually be ruled by fear anxiety and a lack of self-confidence.

Of course, you are worth everything. You are endowed with talents, skills and personality that make you important to those around you and the world. When the voice of the inner critic tells you, you can’t do something or you’re not good enough it’s important to face it with everything you have and prove it wrong.

Keep in mind that we don't always have to be good at everything, so don’t be afraid to try new things. While your inner critic may have the noble intention of keeping you from failing, it can also keep you from succeeding.

Self-image and The Role It Plays In Your Life.

Psychologists and philosophers have scrutinized the true worth of a positive self-image for centuries. Even though there are many arguments as to what self-image is, people will agree that self-image has a lot to do with how people feel about themselves.

Some would say that self-image means how a person views himself in the world. What a person does every day, their job, how they treat others, and how attractive they are to others all hinges on their self-image.

Some people have positive perceptions of themselves, while others do not. It is believed that people who have positive perceptions of themselves have been told they are good, or useful. Those who are constantly told they aren't good or useful, have negative perceptions of themselves.

This leads to another definition of self-image, which is how others view a person. If others don't enjoy a person's company, the person may develop a poor self-image. If other people don't find a person attractive, the person may suffer from poor self-image.

People often put too much emphasis on what others think about them. It is important to remember that one's self-image will change throughout their lifetime. They begin to rely less on what others think about them as they mature and find hobbies and social groups that accept them. Their perception changes as they become more educated. Learning a skill or learning more about the world can have a positive impact on a person's self-esteem.

Sometimes, though, a person needs counseling to develop a positive self-image. This is very common among women and teenagers. Fashion magazines show women that are perfect when in reality they are not. Some women feel they cannot live up to these expectations and become depressed. Teenagers feel the same way when they compare themselves to others in their peer group. Unrealistic comparisons like these are dangerous. They can lead to eating disorders, disruptive behavior, and eventually drug or alcohol abuse. Talking with a therapist can sometimes make a person realize that they don't have to compare themselves to others. Their self-image improves and they can lead happy lives.

Self-image needs to be nurtured. Everyone feels less than perfect sometimes. However, most people recover and go on with their lives, while some can't let go of these bad feelings as easily. Their self-image is so unrealistic, that they make themselves sick and need professional help and advice to gain the strength needed to get past those bad feelings.

Chapter 4

How Self-confidence Can Help You Succeed At Anything.

Where does self-confidence come from? How do we get it? Why don't I have it?
The answer to all of these questions can be answered with one word - YOU!

Self-confidence starts with you and your perception of yourself as well as what other people think about your actions or behavior.

For some of us, a lack of self-confidence only affects our high ambitions. You might have always wanted to get up on stage or to be a professional singer or actor for example. Perhaps your life dream is to travel the world and visit different countries or cities, but you don't have the self-confidence to do it. For others, the problem of self-confidence is much closer to home - in the office, at business meetings, public speaking events or presentations.

Self-confidence issues affect most of us at some time, and we can usually find ways of getting around the problem. Avoidance is one tactic we often use – if we can get out of an intimidating situation we'll make up excuses not to take part. However, there are times when we can't get out of it, or we don't want to. If a lack of self-confidence is preventing you from trying something new, or from succeeding in your working life, it's time to do something about it.

As we have discussed before, the starting point for improving your self-confidence is understanding what causes the problem. Low self-esteem, not believing in yourself or your ability, feeling inadequate compared to your colleagues or friends or maybe some kind of trauma from your childhood are all contributing factors. By examining the reasons for your low self-confidence, you're halfway there!

Taking positive action to overcome your fears is the next step to help boost your self-confidence. A simple way to do this is by taking on small challenges. You have allowed your brain to associate certain events or actions with fear, so you've already pre-empted the outcome of these situations. By taking a small step towards conquering this, you'll find that the result is most likely not as bad as you think you'll probably be surprised about how good you feel and your self-confidence will instantly increase.

When you've completed your first small challenge, congratulate yourself on achieving your aim. A small reward can often help. You're already on the right path to improving your self-confidence, so you're ready to take it to the next level. This doesn't need to be a huge task; you don't want to undo all the good work.

Building up your self-confidence takes time, and while you might want to leap ahead, it can be a good idea to take things slowly at first. Steadily increase the risks you're taking to get your self-confidence to where you want to be. Risk-taking does not, of course, mean jumping off a bridge, but the perceived risk of something happening as a result of your actions is usually the biggest barrier to self-confidence.

Self-confidence problems are common for most people, and there are excellent resources to learn to deal with these issues, but if you do have severe difficulty facing certain situations you should seek professional help.

Chapter 5

Some Simple Steps To Boosting Your Self-esteem And Self-confidence.

The strongest single factor in prosperity consciousness is self-esteem: believing you can do it, believing you deserve it, believing you will get it.
- Jerry Gillies

Self-esteem refers to how you think and feel about yourself. These are thoughts and feelings a person may have, which may it be positive, negative, or mixed about one's self. The more positive these thoughts and feelings are, the higher your self-esteem will be and conversely, the more negative these thoughts and feelings are, the lower your self-esteem will become.

Feeling good about yourself is important as it gives you a sense of control over your life. It can also help make a person feel satisfied in a relationship. With a positive self-identity, a person can set realistic expectations for oneself and pursue goals. Having a negative self-perception, on the other hand, results in a distorted view of one's self, which leads to further lack of self-confidence, poor performance, and depression.

In recent times, low self-esteem has been one of the most popular and frequently invoked psychological explanations for behavioral and social problems. Taking their cue from social commentators and media opinion leaders, people have been willing to accept that a limited sense of self-worth lies behind just about every social and personal ill from drug abuse and delinquency to poverty and business failures. The result has been a huge market for self-help manuals and educational programs.

People who have low self-esteem rely heavily on their day-to-day performances. The positive external experience and encouragements help them to battle the negative feelings that they have about themselves. These negative feelings very often trouble people with low self-esteem. In some situations, feelings of inadequacy torture those who do not have enough confidence about themselves and about what they can do.

There are many known ways to improve one's self-esteem. To boost one's confidence, it may be helpful to practice the following self-improvement techniques and strategies:

Rebutting the inner critic that keeps on sending self-defeating messages;

Practicing the art of self-nurturing; and

Get much-needed help and support from people who are close to you.

The first and the most important step to increasing self-esteem is to tell the inner voice to shut up. The inner voice might say negatively about you. In such a situation, you must praise yourself. Rebutting the inner voice that keeps on criticizing you should be done regularly. However, this step is not enough to develop self-esteem.

The second step that one must initiate on a way to healthy self-esteem is that a person should nurture himself. The most important part of this step is to start treating yourself as a worthwhile person.

Seek out people who make you feel good. Remember that you get to choose your friends so why not choose people who think you're great?

Moreover, both individual and group counseling can help improve self-esteem and self-confidence. Such therapy might include assertiveness training, communication skills, and learning to recognize and understand own emotional responses to others.

Therapy may also explore early and later experiences that contributed to your low self-esteem. Group therapy is particularly effective that it helps to foster trust and build relationships, and encourages a sense of belonging- components that are important for building self-esteem and self-confidence.

Chapter 6

Overcoming A Lack of Self-confidence.

Self-confidence is one thing that most people think other people have except for themselves. As we have discussed before, all of us were endowed with special attributes though we rarely recognize these special gifts in ourselves.

We are all capable of being self-confident. It isn't something that was given to the person sitting next to you and not you even though sometimes it may seem that way. It's something we all have. While you may not possess it at the moment this doesn't mean that you can't develop it.

To overcome low self-confidence you must be able to have faith in yourself. You need to feel good about your being you. This all boils down to appreciating the things that we are capable of doing and accepting the fact that some things just won't change however hard we try changing them.

One good example is a physical condition that you have to struggle with. A couple of things may help you with them but this would not erase the facts that your physical conditions may hamper you from developing your confidence.

Ask yourself, what makes you more confident?

Our standards of confidence will affect virtually all aspects of our happiness. Say, we find more value from being good looking then you should start resolving your low self-confidence by making yourself more beautiful. Luckily, for us, there are various methods of transformation and enhancements.

However, if your standards deal more with the innate beauty a person may have like the goodness of attitude or skills and talents, you may start revamping yourself by strengthening these areas.

Low self-confidence is often aggravated by our failures. Failing is inevitable and it must be dealt with a light heart. If you always take your failures seriously and amplify them by ruminating on your mistakes, then it is likely that you are close to self-destruction. Practice an attitude that celebrates victories but forgets about your stupidities.

People are subject to committing mistakes, you must understand that. Your failures must not be used as an excuse to stop trying. Think of your losses as blessings that you must accept and be thankful that they come across your path. This is one proof that the Creator spends more time on you than you would have first imagined.

Instead of allowing these to trouble you, treat them as your learning grounds for not committing mistakes. Then don't allow these failures to hold back your growth.

You see, in the end, it all lies in the attitude we take to deal things out. We must be very careful with the way we handle things. If we think of ourselves negatively and those feelings interfere with our lives, we will never overcome our lack of self-confidence.

Gaining Self-confidence From Within.

How to get self-confidence is the central issue when tackling the development of self-confidence in an individual who, for long, has believed that his self-worth is deficient.

Those confident individuals can bear themselves better than those who have a lower sense of the "self". They are the achievers, the people in the limelight and the center of society. They walk straight; speak their meanings very well and influence people, both subtly and obviously. In short, they are those who care recognizable even from afar.

Sometimes, self-confident people are very much loved by society. It is maybe due to their charisma or they are, by nature very amiable. However, there are those self-confident individuals who, just by leaving make the room lighter.

These are two very different types of self-confidence. One destroys a person's credibility and the other intensifies his personality. You don't want the consequences of being too confident in yourself that the people no longer view you as effective, instead, they see you as an annoyance to their daily affairs.

Self-confidence comes from within. Outside stimulation may help but it would all still boil down to knowing yourself and using that knowledge to gain confidence.

To get self-confidence, you must realize that your limitations must not limit you and your attributes must not destroy you. Instead, use all of these factors to develop a personality that would be productive for you and all those that surround you.

"Know thyself!", says the Oracle at Delphi. Though this might have been said thousands of years ago, it is undeniably true that we still can use the wisdom it says.

Know yourself and get confidence. Recognize though that knowledge comes nowhere but inside you. Thus, you have to accept the reality that unless you embrace your flaws and perfection, the demons of low self-confidence would stay forever lingering in your being.

There is a great risk in knowing too much of yourself though if your foundations of self-control are not much too developed. You'll be exposed to your imperfections and since control is not yet yours, you may be eaten by your flows. This condition is closely intertwined with thought rumination wherein you seem to go around in your circle of thoughts about your losses and failures regardless of your achievements.

Another danger of having no control over yourself while trying to get self-confidence is that you might get too confident that you would forget the real value of having a sense of self. As we have mentioned earlier, overconfidence is just as dangerous as having no confidence at all. This would send you back to failures or worse to an eventual downfall.

Knowing yourself is one factor that may be either dangerous or productive. Self-awareness often helps people realize how wonderful their creation was. They learn to give worth to their capacities and attributes that are as special as those that may be found in other people. We are all unique and that is a fact. Our marks of uniqueness can be seen by closely looking at our capabilities and our incapacities. Our uniqueness is manifested in the natural gifts that add to our greater self-value. Our uniqueness can be seen through our potential that we may either ignore or maximize at will.

All these are truths that would stay hidden from you unless you have learned to contemplate your being and be aware of who you truly are.

Chapter 7

Some Things That Matter When Building Your Self-confidence.

The man seems to have found many excuses that eventually help him develop insecurities. The sad truth though is that self-confidence is often hard to be achieved and whenever it passes us by, we try to suppress it.

We treat ourselves severely while we give regard to other people. We laugh at our own mistakes while contemplating how stupid we have become. We hate to see ourselves commit errors. We believe that other people can perform better than we can. We say to ourselves that we are ugly and incapable of doing things. The irony though is that people think otherwise. They view us as wonderful people who are worth admiration.

Low self-confidence can hinder us from our growth. It will always pull us down into the realms of mediocre life and dullness. It will make ways so that we would fit in the gaps of the non-achievers, the humiliated and the lowly people. There is no such world but because men tend not to listen to the voices that encourage them to believe in themselves, this world came forth to life.

The thing though is that experience and time are often good teachers if we truly take them as such. We will live with ourselves for as long as we live with them. Our "self" will accompany us through the course of our life. Somehow, we would learn to live with it. To love it and to accept the truth that many things about it do change and develop.

It may not be out of our chronological age that we would mature but the fact is, we would still mature regardless of the time we would take.

Sometimes, development comes out naturally. Sometimes, we would need effective stimulation. Self-confidence roots down from these two.

Development of self-confidence may suddenly dawn on you. The realization would come as if something breathed life into you and awoke you from a long sleep. From your inner self comes the voice that would tell you what to do and how to do them. It would help you see the stock that you have- your talents, your skills, the crafts that you can do, the stuff that you are good at and all the attributes that it can use to positively reinforce you.

This inner voice, in a sense, will lay everything in your front. It is for you to accept that these things are yours and must be used for your development.

But as we have said, it would require stimulation before your belief in yourself materializes.

You may not have noticed it lately but you are talking with yourself. We all do! The difference though lies in the fashion of talking and the words we are uttering.

Self-talk may either be detrimental or positive. Whatever we say to ourselves will be recorded in our unconsciousness. This in turn would rely on more dominant beliefs we record. Thus, we frequently assert that we're worth nothing, or that we are the ugliest person or the illest performing. It would create an environment in ourselves that would be ideal for pulling us down. However, the opposite is also true. We only have to take advantage of positive talk so that we would reap the benefits of self-confidence.

Some Things To Do When Your Confidence Need A Boost

Small changes make a big difference!

It all boils down to a single idea that would recreate your self-image. Remember when you were so confident of having done something then someone commented on how bad things went?

Self-confidence goes hand and hand with positive thinking. If you think positively of yourself and take stock of all the positive attributes you have, your confidence will grow and you will soon begin to realize you can do and can make things happen.

Positive thinking is not being overly hopeful of something unachievable. Central to boosting self-confidence and positive thinking is the setting of realistic goals that you can reach while not delimiting your capacities.

Normally when we set out to do something we tend to over-calculate things and plan to achieve things beyond our present reach. This, we say, would encourage us to work double time. The point we are missing is that once we fail our expectations and the expectations of the crowd that is watching us, we will be discouraged to try things again.

You see, on our initial tries, it is not bad if we would set achievable goals rather than confidence, boosting-unrealistic goals that would leave us dismayed.

When you feel good about yourself, remember that self-confidence is largely controlled by the hormonal balance in your body. Thus, you can alter your mood by stimulating yourself to do so. Say, if you have this vivid memory of having been able to achieve something or you once had "cheerleaders" who pushed you to achieve greater things, you can surely use them to manipulate your emotions. If not, then remember the moments when you felt happy about yourself. Controlling the reins of your moods and emotions can contribute to your overall confidence.

At one point in our lives, we all have been our critics. Undue criticisms don't only make us vulnerable to negative thoughts, they also affect our overall personal perspectives.

Have you noticed how we criticize ourselves without even realizing that we can't utter those very things to other people? We are harsher to ourselves than we can imagine. Thus, with every negative input we receive from this critic, we are left upset and unconfident. It is like tearing down the walls that we have built a foam long in exchange for a few unjust remarks that we rarely need.

Avoid using over-generalization about yourself because these are the very things that would eventually strip you of your good self-image. Recreating the comments you give to yourself will have a huge impact on your self-confidence.

In the end, destruction comes from within us. Other people may argue that we are affected by external pessimism. True, yet this would only affect us once we allow entry towards ourselves. Thus, you only have to create barriers from negative inputs while strengthening your underlying foundations.

Chapter 8

Building Confidence and Self-esteem

Optimism! It all lies in our positive perception of our personality, the events occurring around us, and life itself. So long as we believe in the goodness that we may have in life, we are bound to enjoy it the way every man should.

Unfortunately, many of us cannot grasp optimism from a life that is muddled with misery, self-doubt, and struggle. Of course, life's pleasure would not be appreciated if it were not equaled with unhappiness. Pain can’t be felt if all we know is joy. Tears would lose their worth if we always experience happiness. Confidence would not be recognized if we do not fall flat on our faces sometimes.

Life is a gratifying privilege and we can make everything we want from it. We have to start early in building our foundations so that we won't have to lose precious moments that shall never pass by us again. A moment that's gone is gone forever but your light won't even lose its value long after you have gone.

With optimism in life, we would be able to recognize the fullness of our potential. Everyone has an equal chance for recognition yet many of us fail to share the limelight because we surrender even before the battle begins.

If you would want to share what the world offers, you must be brave enough. Nothing should stop you from living your life, not even the miserable demons of low self-confidence.

Those who braved life are those who are confident enough in themselves. Sometimes, we just have to take risks so that we might discover what lies on our road. Taking risks though requires lots of faith in yourself. Without this, you would be like a warrior who has lost his armor.

From birth, we were equipped with all the skills that we will use in the later stages of our lives. One such skill is the ability to face challenges and to face them with faith, both in ourselves and in Him who has created all of us.

All of us have an equal chance to develop our sense of self, no matter our circumstances.

We normally have the common notion that life is unfair when in fact, it is not. We all have our shares of blessings and our shares of challenges. It just lies in our perception of things and how we handle things.

The same thing goes with self-confidence and self-esteem. Many of us think that the man we are looking up to shares much of life's blessings because he can bear himself better, he can face the public better and he is much more eloquent and more confident than most of us. Remember that before he even got there, he has to face challenges that contributed to his self-esteem and self-confidence. All of us can be that man, only if we believe in ourselves enough.

We just have to find our enlightenment to be able to achieve the building of good foundations for our self-esteem and self-confidence. Changes must come from within before we can accept the assistance that comes from outside. Realization of how valuable you are and how beautifully you were created cannot be helped by outside reinforcement if you, yourself do not want to accept this one truth.

Go on, help in the discovery of yourself and that is among the most wonderful venture you will take in life.

www.ingramcontent.com/pod-product-compliance
Lightning Source LLC
LaVergne TN
LVHW020536160826
845677LV00015B/4098

9798847885713